ittle Mitchie

PLAYING GAMES TOGETHER

MAKING NEW FRIENDS

ANNE ACCARDI

CREATING YOUNG NONFICTION READERS

Little Mitchie books spark curiosity and support early nonfiction reading for students in Grades 2-3. Designed to build vocabulary, support second language learners, and prepare readers for middle-grade content, each book includes helpful tips for parents and educators to build confidence and deepen understanding of the world.

TIPS FOR READING NONFICTION WITH BEGINNING READERS

Talk about Nonfiction

Begin by explaining that nonfiction books give us information that is true. The book will be organized around a specific topic or idea, and we may learn new facts through reading.

Look at the Parts

Most nonfiction books have helpful features. Our *Little Mitchie* titles include color photographs and graphic aids, a table of contents, a glossary, and an index. Share the purpose of these features with your reader.

Color Photos and Graphic Aids

A lot of information can be found by "reading" photos, charts, maps, and other graphic aids found within nonfiction texts. Help your reader learn more about the different ways information can be displayed.

Table of Contents

Located at the front of the book, this list shows the big ideas within the text and the page numbers where they can be found.

Glossary

Located at the back of the book, the glossary defines key words and phrases that are related to the topic. These words and phrases can be found in the text in colored type.

Index

Located at the back of the book, an index is an alphabetical list of topics and the page numbers where they can be found.

With a little help and guidance about reading nonfiction, you can feel good about introducing a young reader to the world of *Little Mitchie* nonfiction books.

Little Mitchie is an imprint of:

Mitchell Lane
PUBLISHERS

2001 SW 31st Avenue
Hallandale, FL 33009
mitchelllanepub.com

First Edition, 2027.

Author: Anne Accardi
Designer: Kathy Walsh
Editor: Kim Thompson

Library of Congress Cataloging-in-Publication Data
Title: Playing Games Together / by Anne Accardi

Description: Hallandale, FL :
Mitchell Lane Publishers, [2027]

Identifiers:
ISBN 979-8-89260-900-5 (library bound)
ISBN 979-8-90145-056-7 (paperback)
ISBN 979-8-90145-004-8 (eBook)

Library of Congress Control Number: 2026931400

Photo credits: Shutterstock: Cover, p 1 & backgrounds, matimix; p 5, PeopleImages; p 7, Sviatlana Yankouskaya; p 8, Victor Canales Studio; p 11, matimix; p 13, Pixel-Shot; p 15, wavebreakmedia; p 17, SeventyFour; p 18, Milijan Zivkovic; p 19, Sergey Novikov; p 21, PeopleImages

TABLE OF CONTENTS

Step One

KNOW WHY PLAYING TOGETHER IS IMPORTANT

One of the best ways to make friends is to play games with other kids. Games are fun and exciting. They bring people together.

You can play sports on a team or in a pickup game. You can play board games, video games, or your own made-up games. You can play at recess, at home, or at the park.

CHALLENGE
Make a list of five games you would like to try. How could you learn each one?

Games teach you to **collaborate** and get along with others. If you and a friend are on the same team, you work together to win. If you play against a friend, you must respect your **opponent**.

"It's not whether you win or lose,
it's how you play the game."
—Grantland Rice

Step Two

FACE YOUR FEARS

You may not know how to play a game that your friends are playing. The best way to learn is to dive in.

Soccer rules or video game menus make the most sense when you are on the field or in the middle of the action. Ask others for tips. Join a team and work hard at practice. You will soon be a skilled player.

FRIENDLY FACT

Making mistakes helps you learn. With **perseverance**, your skills will grow. Along the way, laugh at yourself and have fun!

You may be worried that you won't be included in a game. Ignore groups that **exclude** kids from joining in. Games are more fun when everyone has a chance to play.

FRIENDLY FACT

Playing games helps people know and appreciate each other. It helps bonds form. It's a great way to create a **community**.

Step Three

TAKE ACTION!

Game on! When it's time to play, be sure to play **fair**. Give everyone a turn.

Follow the rules. If needed, agree on rules before the game begins. That will make sure everyone gets along and has fun.

Cheating ruins the fun for everyone. It makes the game unfair. It makes it hard for friends to **trust** each other.

CHALLENGE

Write three words that tell how you feel when someone cheats.

Many games are **competitive**. It is natural to want to win. Remember, though, that being kind and having fun with friends is more important than winning.

Here are a few things to say after a game.

- *Good game!*
- *That was fun.*
- *Thanks for playing with me.*
- *Congratulations on winning!*
- *You played really well.*

Step Four

KEEP GOING

Playing games is a great way to make friends. Keep growing your circle! Invite new people to play. You may find you have a lot in common.

CHALLENGE

Think of someone at school you have never played with. Invite them to play a game with you.

TOP TIPS

Learn by diving in.

Mistakes are okay.

Include everyone.

Play fair.

Have fun!

GLOSSARY

collaborate (kuh-LAB-uh-rate) to work together

community (kuh-MYOO-ni-tee) a group of people who help each other and have things in common

competitive (kuhm-PET-i-tiv) describes a game where some people win and some lose

exclude (ik-SKLOOD) to leave out

fair (fair) reasonable, just, and equal for everyone; by the rules

opponent (uh-POH-nuhnt) a person you are playing against in a game or sport

perseverance (pur-suh-VEER-uhns) continued effort to accomplish something in the face of difficulties

trust (truhst) to believe that someone is honest and reliable

FURTHER READING

Jones, Christianne. *Lucia Lacorte, Poor Sport*. Picture Window Books, 2019.

Philip, Simon. *I Really Want to Win*. Templar Publishing, 2019.

Reed, Charlotte. *Good Game*. Lerner Publications, 2024.

ON THE INTERNET

CBS Mornings: Kindness 101: A Lesson in Sportsmanship
youtube.com/watch?v=ehDVE9QlrqQ
Watch an amazing example of how lives can be changed when friends play together.

National Geographic Kids: How to Be an Awesome Friend
kids.nationalgeographic.com/pages/article/friend
Learn tips for making and keeping friends.

INDEX